SET UP
FOR *Success*

SET SAIL
FOR *Success*

Compiled by **Eric Holmes**

PRODUCTIONS, LLC

Allen, Texas

www.SetSailforSuccess.com

Book Design: Masciarelli Design
www.masciarellidesign.com

Printed in the United States of America

ISBN: 0-9747837-0-6

Contents

INTRODUCTION

Numerous studies have defined success in many ways. Remarkably they all gravitate to one answer and that is only about five percent of people are successful. Their reason that only one out of twenty people can be successful is that success, however you define it, is a lot of hard work.

First, you have to have a clear vision of exactly what you want to achieve. This has to be something very clear in your mind and something you will become willing to work for persistently and patiently. You must dream a great dream and make it a dedication for your life. It can be anything as long as it is yours.

Second, you must realize that to go from where you are now to the fulfillment of your dream you need a roadmap. You need a realistic plan that lays out goals along the way and creates a timeline for each *step. A little planning up front will make the difference in your final success. Formulate a plan and make adjustments and refinements as you go. If you have a dream, then you owe it to yourself to create the roadmap.*

Now all that's left to do is to execute on the plan. This is simple for some and for others this is very difficult. Changing your life is an emotional event and can cause you to become uncomfortable. You may need a whole new support network. It is also possible that you will have a fear of success. Your present self will try to hold you down. If this becomes stressful then remember the goal and just concentrate on one task at a time as required by the plan. Follow your plan like a recipe. Take it one step at a time.

If you can dream a great dream, plan your journey, and then do each step required along the way you can be part of that five percent!

DREAM

If you follow your bliss,
    doors will open for you
        that wouldn't have opened for anyone else.
                                Joseph Campbell

You can do anything you wish to do,
    have anything you wish to have,
    be anything you wish to be.

                                Robert Collier

It takes a person with a mission to succeed.
                                Clarence Thomas

If one *advances*

CONFIDENTLY

in the direction of

his *dreams,*
and endeavors

to live a life which

*he has **imagined,***

HE WILL MEET with

a *success u n e x p e c t e d*

in common hours.

Henry David Thoreau

Live your beliefs
    and you can turn
    your world around.

Henry David Thoreau

Cherish your visions and your dreams,
    as they are the children of your soul;
    the blueprints of your
    ultimate achievements.

Napoleon Hill

Life is what your thoughts make it.

Marcus Aurelius

We grow *great*
by DREAMS.
All big men are DREAMERS.
They *see* things in
the s o f t h a z e of a spring day or
in *the red fire* of
a LONG winter's evening.
Some of us let
these *great dreams* die,
but others *nourish* and *protect* them;
nurse them
THROUGH bad days till
they bring them to
the SUNSHINE and LIGHT which
c o m e s a l w a y s to those who
SINCERELY HOPE
that their D REAM S
will come true.

Woodrow Wilson

No person has the right
   to rain on your dreams.

Marian Wright Edelman

See things
   as you would have them
   be instead of as they are.

Robert Collier

Figure out where
   your passions lie,
   and realign
   your priorities accordingly.

Cord Cooper

Somehow I CAN'T BELIEVE
there are many heights
that CAN'T BE SCALED
by a man
who *knows* the *secret* of
making dreams come true.

This special *secret*
can be SUMMARIZED in four C's.
They are:
CURIOSITY,
CONFIDENCE,
COURAGE,
AND
CONSTANCY,
and the *greatest* of these
is
CONFIDENCE.

Walt Disney

Your imagination
is your preview of
life's coming attractions.

Albert Einstein

A man is but the product of his thoughts.
What he thinks, he becomes.

Mohandas Gandhi

To understand the heart and mind
of a person,
look not at what he has already achieved,
but at what he aspires to.

Kahlil Gibran

Nothing is
AS REAL AS
a *dream*.
The *world* can
CHANGE around you,
BUT
*your **dream** will **not**.*

RESPONSIBILITIES
need
not erase it.
DUTIES
need
not obscure it.

Because
the ***dream*** is *within* you,
no one can take it
away.

Tom Clancy

17

You can achieve what
   your mind can conceive.

Napoleon Hill

Man's mind, once
   stretched by a new idea,
   never regains
   its original dimension.

Oliver Wendell Holmes

An invasion of armies
   can be resisted
   but not an idea
   whose time has come.

Victor Hugo

What every man needs,
regardless of his job or
the *kind* of work he is doing,
is a VISION of *what*
his place *is* and may *be*.

He needs an OBJECTIVE
and a PURPOSE.
He needs a *feeling* and a BELIEF
that he has some WORTHWHILE
thing to do.

What this is *no one* can tell him.
It must be his *OWN* creation.
Its success WILL BE MEASURED
by the *nature* of his vision,
what he *has done* to equip himself,
and *how well* he has performed
ALONG the line of its *development*.

Joseph M. Dodge

All men of action
   are dreamers.

James G. Huneker

All human beings
   are also dream beings.
   Dreaming ties
   all mankind together.

Jack Kerouac

Everything you can imagine
   is real.

Pablo Picasso

· D R E A M ·

PROVIDENCE
has nothing
good or *high*
in store for one
who does not
resolutely aim at
something
high or *good*.
A PURPOSE
is
THE ETERNAL CONDITION
of *success*.

Thornton T. Munger

Man is not the sum of what he has
  but the totality of what he does
  not yet have,
  of what he might have.

Jean-Paul Sartre

The indispensable first step
  to getting the things
  you want out of life is this:
  decide what you want.

Ben Stein

Dreams are the touchstones
  of our character.

Henry David Thoreau

FORMULATE and STAMP
indelibly on
your mind
a MENTAL PICTURE of
yourself
SUCCEEDING.
Hold
this picture
TENACIOUSLY.

Never
permit it
to *fade.*
Your mind
will seek
to develop
this picture.

Norman Vincent Peale

Dreams come true;
  without that possibility,
  nature would not incite us
  to have them.

John Updike

Don't ever let anyone
  steal your dreams.

Dexter Yager

One man has enthusiasm for thirty minutes,
  another for thirty days,
  but it is the man who has it
  for thirty years
  who makes a success of his life.

Edward B. Butler

When you DETERMINED
what
you want,
you have made
the *most*
important decision
of YOUR LIFE.

You have to know
what
you want in order
to ATTAIN it.

Douglas Lurtan

First say to yourself
   what you would be;
   and then do
   what you have to do.

Epictetus

To accomplish great things,
   we must not only act,
   but also dream;
   not only plan,
   but also believe.

Anatole France

By your thoughts you are daily,
   even hourly, building your life;
   you are carving your destiny.

Ruth Barrack Golden

DO NOT FOLLOW
where
the path
may lead.
GO instead
where
there is no path
and LEAVE A TRAIL.
Only *those*
who WILL RISK
going *too far*
can possibly
find out how far
one
can go.

T. S. Elliot

I always have to dream up there
    against the stars.
    If I don't dream I will make it,
    I won't even get close.

Henry J. Kaiser

Instead of thinking about
    where you are, think about
    where you want to be.
    It takes twenty years of hard work
    to become an overnight success.

Diana Rankin

There are those that look at things
    the way they are, and ask why?
    I dream of things that never were,
    and ask why not.

George Bernard Shaw

We need to give
OURSELVES
permission *to act out*
our *dreams* and visions,
not look for
more SENSATIONS,
more PHENOMENA,
but live
our strongest
dreams
-- even if *it takes*
a lifetime.

Vijali Hamilton

An idea is never given to you
without you being given
the power to make it reality.

Richard Bach

We are what we think.
All that we are arises with our thoughts.
With our thoughts,
we make the world.

Buddha

Great hopes make everything possible
Benjamin Franklin

DETERMINE
what
specific goal
you want
to achieve.

Then
DEDICATE YOURSELF
to
its
attainment

with unswerving singleness
of purpose,
the trenchant
zeal of
a crusader.

Paul J. Meyer

You have brains in your head.
 You have feet in your shoes.
 You can steer yourself
 in any direction you choose.

Dr. Seuss

What is now proved
 was once only imagined.

William Blake

I have heard it said
 that the first ingredient of success
 -- the earliest spark in
 the dreaming youth -- is this;
 dream a great dream.

John Appleman

Aim for your *star,*
no matter HOW FAR, you must reach
high above
and *touch* your life
WITH LOVE,
you must never
look back, but *charge on!*
Attack!

SEE your **goal**
your star of *desire,*
SEE IT RED HOT,
feel it burning,
you must be obsessed with it
to make it your *true* yearning,
be READY my friends for
when you **truly** *believe it,*
you will certainly achieve it
and by all of GOD'S UNIVERSAL LAWS
you *will always* receive it!

Bob Smith

Nothing great has ever been achieved
except by those who dared
believe something inside them
was superior to circumstances.

Bruce Barton

No bird soars too high
if he soars
with his own wings.

William Blake

The moment of enlightenment is
when a person's dreams of possibilities
become images of probabilities.

Vic Braden

When we are motivated

by *goals* that have *deep* meaning,

by *dreams*
that need *completion*,

by *pure love*
that needs *expressing*,

THEN

we truly live life.

Greg Anderson

Ah, but a man's reach
should exceed his grasp
– or what's a heaven for?

Robert Browning

Don't be afraid of the space between
your dreams and reality.
If you can dream it,
you can make it so.

Belva Davis

Man is truly great
when he acts from his passions.

Benjamin Disraeli

Make no
L I T T L E plans,
they have
no magic
to S T I R men's blood
and *will not*
be realized.

Make big plans;
aim high
in *hope* and *work*,
R E M E M B E R I N G that
a **noble** and **logical** plan
never dies,
but
L O N G A F T E R W E A R E G O N E
will be a living thing.

Lita Bane

It is difficult to say what is impossible,
  for the dream of yesterday
  is the hope of today
  and the reality of tomorrow.

Robert H. Goddard

Dream no small dreams
  for they have no power
  to move the hearts of men.

Johann Wolfgang von Goethe

It's time to start living
  the life we have imagined.

Henry James

The **more**
you can *tap* into
your ***dreams***
the **more**
you can
i n c r e a s e
your chances of
BEING ABLE
at last
to do
w h a t you
ALWAYS
wanted **to do**
with
your life.

Richard Nelson Bolles

Only things the dreamers make live on.
  They are the eternal conquerors.

Herbert Kaufman

And the day came
  when the risk to remain tight in a bud
  was more painful than
  the risk it took to blossom.

Anais Nin

Everything starts
  as somebody's day dream.

Larry Niven

The FIRST glance
at *History*
convinces us that
the *actions* of men
proceed from
their *needs*,
their *passions*,
their *characters*
and
talents;
and
impresses us with
the **belief**
that such
needs,
passions and
interests
are the **sole spring**
of ACTIONS.

Georg Hegel

At first our dreams seem impossible,
then they seem improbable,
but when we summon the will,
they become inevitable.

Christopher Reeve

Dream lofty dreams, and as you dream,
so shall you become.
Your vision is the promise of
what you shall at last unveil.

John Ruskin

Nothing happens unless first a dream.

Carl Sandburg

In times when
the *passions* are beginning
TO TAKE CHARGE of
the *conduct*
of human affairs,
ONE should pay
less attention to
WHAT men of **experience**
and **common sense**
are thinking
than to
WHAT is preoccupying
the IMAGINATION
of
dreamers.

Alexis de Tocqueville

We are such stuff as dreams are made on.

William Shakespeare

Reach high, for
stars lie hidden in your soul.
Dream deep,
for every dream precedes the goal.

Pamela Vaull Starr

Dreams are renewable.
No matter what our age or condition,
there are still untapped possibilities
within us and a new beauty
waiting to be born.

Dale Turner, PhD

When you are inspired
by some **great** purpose,
some EXTRAORDINARY project,
all your thoughts
b r e a k their bounds:
Your mind transcends

L I M I T A T I O N S,

your consciousness

E X P A N D S

in every direction,
and you find *y o u r s e l f*
in a ***new***,
great, and
wonderful world.

Pantanjali

A man's dreams are an index
to his greatness.

Zadoc Rabinowitz

Dream big and dare to fail.

Norman D. Vaughan

The very least you can do in your life
is to figure out what you hope for.
And the most you can do
is live inside that hope.
Not admire it from a distance
but live right in it, under its roof.

Barbara Kingsolver

It's not
WHAT'S **happening**
to *you* now or
WHAT **has happened**
in your past that
DETERMINES
who you become.
Rather, it's
your decisions
about what **TO FOCUS ON**,
what things **MEAN** to you,
and **what** you're going
to *do* about them
that **WILL DETERMINE**
your ultimate
DESTINY.

Anthony Robbins

A soul without a high aim
is like a ship without a rudder.

Eileen Caddy

The tragedy of life is not so much
what men suffer,
but rather what they miss.

Thomas Carlyle

Hold fast to dreams for if dreams die,
life is a broken-winged bird
that cannot fly.

Langston Hughes

One day
ALICE came to a *fork*
in the road
and saw a **Cheshire cat** in a tree.

*"Which **road** do I take?"*
she asked.
*"**Where** do you want to go?"*
was his response.
*"I **don't** know,"*
Alice answered.
"Then,"
said the cat,
*"it **doesn't** matter."*

Lewis Carroll

The poor man is not
   he who is without a cent,
   but he who is without a dream.

Harry Kemp

Life is real! Life is earnest!
   And the grave is not its goal.

Henry Wadsworth Longfellow

The greatest danger for most of us
   is not that our aim is too high
   and we miss it,
   but that our aim is too low
   and we hit it.

Tim Timmons

You are not here
MERELY
to make a living.
You are here in order
to enable the world
to live more AMPLY,
with *greater* vision,
with a *finer* spirit
of *hope*
and ACHIEVEMENT.
You are here
to **enrich** the world,
and you
impoverish yourself
IF
you forget the errand.

Woodrow Wilson

Keep away from people who try
to belittle your ambitions.
Small people always do that,
but the really great
make you feel that you, too,
can become great.

Mark Twain

Goals. There's no telling what you can do
when you get inspired by them.
There's no telling what you can do
when you believe in them.
There's no telling what will happen
when you act upon them.

Jim Rohn

Youth is not ENTIRELY
a *time* of life;
it is a *state of mind*.
Nobody **grows old**
by merely living
a NUMBER of years.
People **grow old**
by *deserting* their ideals.
You are
as YOUNG as your FAITH,
as OLD as your DOUBTS;
as YOUNG as your SELF-CONFIDENCE,
as OLD as your FEAR;
as YOUNG as your HOPE,
as OLD as your DESPAIR.

Douglas MacArthur

A man is not old until regrets
   take the place of dreams.

John Barrymore

Don't part with your illusions.
   When they are gone you may still exist,
   but you have ceased to live.

Mark Twain

Twenty years from now
   you will be more disappointed
   by the things that you didn't do
   than by the ones you did do.
   So throw off the bowlines.
   Sail away from the safe harbor.
   Catch the trade winds in your sails.
   Explore. Dream. Discover.

Mark Twain

The **only true** measure
of *success*
is
the ***ratio*** between
what we might have done
and
what we might have been
on the one hand,
and **the thing**
WE HAVE MADE
and **the things**
WE HAVE MADE
OF *ourselves*
on the other.

H.G. Wells

PLAN

A plan is a list of actions
   arranged in whatever sequence is
   thought likely
   to achieve an objective.

John Argenti

It's not the plan that is important;
   it's the planning.

Graeme Edwards

Great things are not done by impulse,
   but by a series of small things
   brought together.

Vincent Van Gogh

Having an
EXCITING destination
is like
setting a needle
in your **compass**.
From then on,
the **compass** knows only
one point-its ideal.
And it will
FAITHFULLY
guide you *there*
through
the **darkest** nights
and **fiercest** storms.

Daniel Boone

First comes thought;
    then organization of that thought,
    into ideas and plans;
    then transformation of those plans
    into reality.

Napoleon Hill

People talk fundamentals
    and superlatives and
    then make some changes in detail.

Oliver Wendell Holmes, Jr.

The primary questions for an adult
    are not why or how,
    but when and where.

Eugen Rosenstock-Huessy

We cannot SEEK
or ATTAIN
health,
wealth,
learning,
JUSTICE or
kindness
in general.
Action is always
s p e c i f i c,
C O N C R E T E ,
I N D I V I D U A L I Z E D,
unique.

John Dewey

By failing to plan
   we are planning to fail.

Brian Tracy

The simple joy of taking
   an idea into one's own hands and
   giving it proper form, that's exciting.

George Nelson

A good plan is like a road map:
   it shows the final destination and
   usually the best way to get there.

H. Stanley Judd

THOROUGHNESS
characterizes
all successful men.
Genius
is the *art* of taking
INFINITE
pains.
All great achievement
has been
characterized by
extreme care,
INFINITE PAINSTAKING,
even
to the
minutest detail.

Elbert Hubbard

The shortest distance between two points
  is under construction.

Noelie Alito

If you cry "Forward!"
  you must without fail make plain
  in what direction to go.

Anton Chekhov

Always have a plan,
  and believe in it.
  Nothing happens by accident.

Chuck Knox

A cripple
in the *right* way
may **beat** a racer
in the *wrong* one.
Nay,
the *fleeter*
and *better*
the racer is,
who hath once
missed
HIS WAY,
the *farther*
he leaveth
behind.

Sir Francis Bacon

I am tomorrow, or some future day,
  what I establish today.
  I am today what I established yesterday
  or some previous day.

Harvey Spencer Lewis

Reduce your plan to writing...
  The moment you complete this,
  you will have definitely given
  concrete form to the intangible desire.

Napoleon Hill

Making the simple complicated
  is commonplace;
  making the complicated simple,
  awesomely simple, that's creativity.

Charles Mingus

The great *successful* men
of the WORLD
have used their
imagination...
they THINK AHEAD
and *create*
their mental picture
in all its details,
filling in here,
adding a little there,
altering **this** a bit
and **that** a bit,
but STEADILY building
- STEADILY building.

Robert Collier

It's not the load
that breaks you down,
it's the way you carry it.

Lena Horne

Developing the plan
is actually laying out
the sequence of events
that have to occur
for you to achieve your goal.

George L. Morrisey

Every man is the architect
of his own fortune.

Appius Claudius

The reason most people
never *reach* their goals
is that they don't
DEFINE them,
LEARN about them,
or even seriously
CONSIDER them as
believable or *achievable*.
WINNERS can tell you
where they are going,
what they plan to do
ALONG the way,
and **who** will be sharing
the *adventure*
with them.

Denis Waitley

Let our advance worrying
   become advance thinking and planning.
                    Sir Winston Churchill

In action be primitive;
   in foresight, a strategist.

                              Rene Char

Follow effective action
   with quiet reflection.
   From the quiet reflection
   will come even
   more effective action.

                              James Levin

Every
minute
you spend
in *planning*
SAVES
10 minutes
in *execution*;
this
GIVES YOU
a 1,000
PERCENT
return on
energy!

Brian Tracy

Let us watch well our beginnings,
and results will manage themselves.

Alexander Clark

Setting a goal is not the main thing.
It is deciding how you will go
about achieving it
and staying with that plan.

Tom Landry

We're all pilgrims on the same journey
-but some pilgrims
have better road maps.

Nelson Demille

If you don't
DESIGN
your own
life plan,
chances are
you'll
fall
into
someone else's plan.
And GUESS WHAT
they have *planned*
for you?
Not much.

Jim Rohn

Few people have any next,
  they live from hand to mouth
  without a plan,
  and are always
  at the end of their line.

Ralph Waldo Emerson

Learn to see in another's calamity
  the ills that you should avoid.

Thomas Jefferson

Organizing is what you do
  before you do something,
  so that when you do it,
  it is not all mixed up.

A. A. Milne

There are
those
who **travel**
and
those
who a**re going**
SOMEWHERE.
They are *different*
and yet they are *the same*.
The *success*
has this over
his *rivals:*
He KNOWS
where
he is
going.

Mark Caine

Spectacular achievement
is always preceded by
spectacular preparation.

Robert H. Schuller

Whether or not
you reach your goals in life
depends entirely on how well
you prepare for them and
how badly you want them.

Ronald McNair

Success depends upon previous preparation,
and without such preparation
there is sure to be failure.

Confucius

One essential
to *success*
is that
your DESIRE
be an *all-obsessing* one,
your THOUGHTS
and AIMS
be *co-ordinate*,
and your ENERGY
be *concentrated*
and *applied*
WITHOUT
let up.

Claude M. Bristol

When you're prepared,
you're more confident.
When you have a strategy,
you're more comfortable.

Fred Couples

Winning can be defined
as the science of being
totally prepared.

George Allen

Don't expect mangoes
when you plant papayas.

Mimfa A. Gibson

Most of us
serve
our **ideals** by
FITS and STARTS.
The person
who MAKES
a success of living
is **one**
who **sees**
his *goal*
STEADILY
and **aims** for it
UNSWERVINGLY.
That's
dedication.

Cecil B. DeMille

Forewarned is forearmed.
   To be prepared is half the victory.
                              Miguel de Cervantes

The will to succeed is important,
   but what's even more important
   is the will to prepare.

                              Bobby Knight

In the fields of observation
   chance favors only the prepared mind.

                              Louis Pasteur

I FEEL that
the *most* important step
in any major
ACCOMPLISHMENT
is setting
a *specific goal*.
This ENABLES you
to *keep* your mind
focused on your goal
and off the many obstacles
that *will arise*
when you're STRIVING
to do
your best.

Kurt Thomas

Trust in your preparation.

Davie Sheppard

The loftier the building
   the deeper
   the foundation must be.

Thomas A. Kempis

Success generally depends upon
   knowing how long
   it takes to succeed.

Baron de Montesquieu

To will is
to *select* a goal,
DETERMINE
a course
of action
that will bring
one
to that *goal,*
and then hold
to **that action**
until
the *goal*
IS REACHED.
The key
is
action.

Michael Hanson

Chance does nothing that
    has not been prepared
    before hand.

Alexis de Tocqueville

Until you identify the obstacles
    that stand between you
    and reaching your objectives,
    you are in denial.

Zig Zigler

Success often comes
    to those who have the aptitude
    to see way down the road.

Laing Burns, Jr.

Our goals
can only
be REACHED
through a *vehicle*
of a PLAN,
in which *we must*
fervently
believe,
and upon which
we must
vigorously
act.
There is **no** other
ROUTE
to *success*.

Stephen A. Brennan

Your goals are the road maps
that guide you and show you
what is possible for your life.

Les Brown

A man without a goal
is like a ship without a rudder.

Thomas Carlyle

By recording your dreams
and goals on paper,
you set in motion the process
of becoming the person
you most want to be.

Mark Victor Hansen

GOALS are
a *means*
to an end,
not the
ULTIMATE PURPOSE
of *our lives*.
They are
simply
a *tool*
to concentrate
our focus
and
MOVE US
in a
direction.

Anthony Robbins

We all need lots of powerful
   long-range goals
   to help us past the short-term obstacles.

Jim Rohn

In every enterprise
   consider where
   you would come out.

Publilius Syrus

If you don't know
   where you are going,
   you'll probably end up
   somewhere else.

Lewis Carroll

FIXING
your *objective*
is like
i d e n t i f y i n g
the NORTH STAR
– you sight
your COMPASS
on it
and then
use it as
the MEANS
of *getting back*
on track
when you *tend*
to s t r a y.

Marshall Dimock

Without goals,
and plans to reach them,
you are like a ship
that has set sail
with no destination.

Fitzhugh Dodson

Never confuse motion
with action.

Ernest Hemingway

Those who give too much attention
to trifling things
become generally incapable
of great things.

Francois de la Rochefoucauld

We succeed
ONLY
as we identify
in LIFE,
or in WAR,
or in ANYTHING ELSE,
a
single
overriding *objective*,
and make
all other
CONSIDERATIONS
bend
to that
one
objective.

Dwight David Eisenhower

Our plans miscarry
    because they have no aim.
When a man does not know
    what harbor he is making for,
no wind is the right wind.

             Lucius Annaeus Seneca

To do two things at once
    is to do neither.

                  Publius Syrus

In the long run men hit only
    what they aim at.

             Henry David Thoreau

One principle
reason
WHY
men are so often
useless
is
that they
D I V I D E
and
s h i f t
their attention
A M O N G
a **multiplicity**
of *o b j e c t s*
and *pursuits.*

G. Emmons

It is the direction
and not the magnitude
which is to be taken
into consideration.

Thomas Troward

The world turns aside
to let any man pass
who knows whither
he is going.

David Starr Jordan

We must ask where we are
and whither we are tending.

Abraham Lincoln

To solve
a **problem** or
to REACH
a goal, you...
don't need
to know
all the answers
in a d v a n c e.
But you *must* have
a clear idea of
the PROBLEM
or the **GOAL**
you want
to **r e a c h**.

W. Clement Stone

The shorter way to do many things
    is to do only one thing at a time.

Wolfgang Amadeus Mozart

Nothing can add
    more power to your life
    than concentrating all your energies
    on a limited set of targets.

Nido Qubein

I am a slow walker,
    but I never walk backwards.

Abraham Lincoln

I respect the man
who *knows* distinctly
what he wishes.
The greater part of
all mischief in the world
ARISES from the fact
that men
do not
sufficiently *understand*
their OWN AIMS.
They have undertaken
to build a tower,
and spend *no more labor*
on the FOUNDATION
than would be **necessary**
to erect a *hut*.

Johann Wolfgang von Goethe

We may not arrive at our port
within a calculable period,
but we should preserve
the true course.

Henry David Thoreau

You will never "find" time for anything.
If you want time you must make it.

Charles Buxton

Time is the scarcest resource,
and unless it is managed,
nothing else can be managed.

Peter Drucker

BEFORE you
begin a thing,
remind yourself
that DIFFICULTIES
and DELAYS
quite impossible to **foresee**
are a h e a d.
…You can ONLY see
one thing CLEARLY, and that
is *your goal.*
Form a mental **vision**
of that
and CLING TO IT
through
thick and *thin.*

Kathleen Norris

Most misfortunes are
the result of misused time.

Napoleon Hill

It takes time to save time.

Joe Taylor

Long is the road
from conception to completion.

Molière

The human mind
is not
RICH enough
to *drive*
many horses
abreast
and *wants*
one GENERAL scheme,
under *which*
it strives
to BRING
everything.

George Santayana

Whoever wants to reach a distant goal
must take small steps.

Helmut Schmidt

If you have built castles in the air,
your work need not be lost;
that is where they should be.
Now put the foundations under them.

Henry David Thoreau

Any plan is bad
which is incapable of modification.

Publilius Syrus

A **young** person,
TO ACHIEVE,
must first
get out
of his mind
any notion
either of
the *ease*
or *rapidity*
of **success**.
NOTHING ever
just **HAPPENS**
in this *world*.

Edward William Bok

Do

I have never heard anything
about the resolutions of the apostles,
but a good deal about their acts.

Horace Mann

The time for action is now.
It's never too late to do something.

Carl Sandburg

Everything you want is out there
waiting for you to ask.
Everything you want also wants you.
But you have to take action to get it.

Jack Canfield

The chief condition
on which,
LIFE,
HEALTH
and VIGOR
depend on,
is *action*.
It is by *action*
that an **organism**
develops its faculties,
increases its energy,
and *attains*
the FULFILLMENT
of its
destiny.

Pierre Joseph Proudhon

A man is the sum of his actions,
of what he has done,
of what he can do, nothing else.
Mohandas Gandhi

Thought and theory must precede
all salutary action;
yet action is nobler in itself
than either thought or theory.
William Wordsworth

You must take action now
that will move you
towards your goals.
Develop a sense of urgency
in your life.

Les Brown

I will act *now*
for *now* is *all* I have.
Tomorrow is the day reserved
for the *labor of the lazy.*
I am *not lazy.*
Tomorrow is the day
when the *failure **will** succeed.*
I am *not a failure.*
I *will act* NOW.
Success will not wait.
If I **delay**,
success will become
wed to another and
lost to me forever.
THIS IS the **time**.
THIS IS the **place**.
I am the person.

Og Mandino

Speak out in acts;
    the time for words has passed,
    and only deeds will suffice.

John Greenleaf Whittier

The secret of getting
    things done is to act!

Benjamin O. David

The difficulties you meet
    will resolve themselves
    as you advance.
    Proceed, and light will dawn,
    and shine with increasing
    clearness on your path.

Jean Le Rond d'Alembert

Everyone who has ever
taken a *shower*
has an IDEA.
It's the person
who
GETS OUT
of the shower,
DRIES OFF
and
DOES
SOMETHING ABOUT IT
who
makes
a *difference*.

Nolan Bushnell

The purest of intentions,
the finest sense of devotion,
the noblest spiritual aspirations
are fatuous
when not realized in action.

Abraham Joshua Heschel

It is easy to sit up and take notice.
What is difficult is getting up
and taking action.

Al Batt

The elevator to success
is out of order.
You'll have to use the stairs…
one step at a time.

Joe Girard

Being **stuck** is
A POSITION **few of us like**.
We want something *new*
but ***cannot*** *let go*
of the OLD
-- OLD IDEAS,
BELIEFS,
HABITS,
even THOUGHTS.
We are **out**
of contact with
our ***own*** *genius*.
Sometimes **we know** we are stuck;
sometimes **we don't**.
In *both* cases
WE HAVE
TO DO SOMETHING.

Inga Teekens

Nothing is impossible
  to the man who can will,
  and then do;
  this is the only law of success.

Mirabeau

Success is the sum of small efforts,
  repeated day in and day out.

Robert Collier

The secret of success
  is constancy to purpose.

Benjamin Disraeli

Often the **difference**
between
a *successful* person
and a *failure*
is not
one has *better*
ABILITIES or IDEAS,
but the COURAGE
that *one* has to bet
on *one's ideas*,
to **take**
a CALCULATED RISK
-- and to act.

Maxwell Maltz

Successful people are successful
  because they form the habits of
  doing those things
  that failures don't like to do.

Albert Gray

Everyone who got where he is
  had to begin where he was.

Robert Louis Stevenson

I know the price of success:
  dedication, hard work
  and unremitting devotion
  to the things you want
  to see happen.

Frank Lloyd Wright

Success *or* failure

depends more upon

ATTITUDE

than upon

CAPACITY.

Successful men

act as though

they have ACCOMPLISHED

or ARE ENJOYING something.

Soon *it becomes* a REALITY.

Act,

look,

feel successful,

conduct yourself accordingly,

and you will be AMAZED

at the positive results.

Dupree Jordan

The path to success is to take massive,
   determined action.

Anthony Robbins

Nothing worthwhile comes easily.
   Work, continuous work and hard work,
   is the only way
   to accomplish results that last.

Hamilton Holt

Successful people are not gifted;
   they just work hard,
   then succeed on purpose.

G. K. Nielson

Most *successful* men
have **not**
achieved
their DISTINCTION
by having
some new talent
or *opportunity*
presented to them.
They HAVE DEVELOPED
the opportunity
that *was*
at *hand.*

Bruce Barton

Plough deep while sluggards sleep.
Benjamin Franklin

Life leaps like a geyser
for those who drill
through the rock of inertia.
Alexis Carrel

Ideas must work through
the brains and the arms
of good and brave men,
or they are no better than dreams.
Ralph Waldo Emerson

I'VE LEARNED that
the resources we need
to *turn*
our dreams
into REALITY
are **within us**,
merely
waiting for
the day when
WE DECIDE
to *wake up*
and *claim*
our
BIRTHRIGHT.

Anthony Robbins

The shortest answer is doing the thing.
George Herbert

This body, full of faults,
  has yet one great quality:
  Whatever it encounters
  in this temporal life
  depends upon one's actions.
Siddha Nagarjuna

An ounce of action is worth a ton of theory.
Friedrich Engels

If your *dream*
is
a ***big*** *dream*,
and if you *want*

YOUR LIFE

to work on
the high level

that you say
you do,

there's no way around
doing the **WORK**

it takes

to *get you* ***there***.

Joyce Chapman

To begin, begin.

Peter Nivio Zarlenga

The secret of getting ahead
is getting started.

Sally Berger

Everyone who got where he is
had to begin where he was.

Richard L. Evans

BEGIN doing
what
you *want*
to do ***now***.
We are **not** living
in ETERNITY.
We have ***only***
this moment,
SPARKLING like
a *star*
in ***our*** hand
-- and m e l t i n g like
a *snowflake*.

Marie Beyon Ray

The beginning is the most
   important part of the work.

Plato

So many fail because
   they don't get started
   -- they don't go.
   They don't overcome inertia.
   They don't begin.

W. Clement Stone

Start by doing what is necessary,
   then do what is possible,
   and suddenly
   you are doing the impossible.

Saint Francis of Assisi

Do not wait;
the *time*
will never be
"JUST RIGHT."
Start
where you stand,
and **work**
with whatever
tools
you may have at
your command,
and ***better tools***
will be found
AS YOU GO ALONG.

Napoleon Hill

Begin -- to begin is half the work,
   let half still remain;
   again begin this, and
   thou wilt have finished.

                 Decimus Magnus Ausonius

It is the job that's never started
   that takes the longest to finish.

                 J. R. R. Tolkien

If you could get up
   the courage to begin,
   you have the courage to succeed.

                 David Viscott

Are you
in *earnest?*
Seize **this** very minute!
Boldness
has *genius,*
power,
and magic in it.
Only ENGAGE,
and then the *mind*
grows **heated**.
Begin,
and then the WORK
will be
COMPLETED.

John Anster

A journey of a thousand miles
starts with a single step.

Lao Tsu

What saves a man
is to take a step.
Then another step.

Antoine de Saint-Exupery

Each step upward
makes me feel stronger
and fit for the next step.

Mohandas Gandhi

All **great** masters
are chiefly
DISTINGUISHED
by the *power* of
adding a **second**,
a **third**, and perhaps
a **fourth** step
in a *continuous* line.
Many a man
has taken
the *first* step.
With EVERY ADDITIONAL STEP
you enhance
immensely
the *value*
of your *first*.

Ralph Waldo Emerson

Diligence overcomes difficulties;
　sloth makes them.

Benjamin Franklin

He who labors diligently
　need never despair;
　for all things are accomplished
　by diligence and labor.

Menander

You can't aim a duck to death.

Gael Boardman

I FIND THE great thing
in this *world*
is not so much
where we stand,
as in *what direction*
we are moving:
TO REACH
the *port of heaven,*
WE MUST SAIL
sometimes with the *wind*
and sometimes *against it,*
but WE MUST SAIL,
and **NOT DRIFT,**
NOR LIE at anchor.

Oliver Wendell Holmes

Be always sure you're right
— then go ahead.

David Crockett

Our grand business is not
to see what lies dimly at a distance,
but to do
what lies clearly at hand.

Thomas Carlyle

A new idea is like a child.
It's easier to conceive
than to deliver.

Ted Koysis

It is **not** good
enough
for *things*
TO BE PLANNED
-- they *still* have
TO **BE DONE**;
for the *intention*
to become
a REALITY,
energy
has to be
launched
into operation.

Pir Vilayat Khan

No sooner said than done
-- so acts your man of worth.

Quintus Ennius

Well done is better
than well said.

Benjamin Franklin

Give me the ready hand
rather than the ready tongue.

Giuseppe Garibaldi

He *who*
EVERY morning
plans
the transactions of the day
and *follows*
THAT **plan**
carries thread
that WILL GUIDE him
through
the labyrinth
of the most
busy
life.

Victor Hugo

Determine never to be idle.
It is wonderful how much
may be done
if we are always doing.

Thomas Jefferson

Get action.
Do things; be sane,
don't fritter away your time…
take a place wherever you are
and be somebody;
get action.

Theodore Roosevelt

Things don't turn up in this world
until somebody turns them up.

James Garfield

My philosophy
on LIFE is that
if we make up
our minds
WHAT we are going
to make of OUR LIVES,
then ***work*** toward
that goal,
we **never lose**
– somehow
we ***win out***.

Ronald Reagan

Even if you are on the right track,
    you will get run over
    if you just sit there.

Will Rogers

If your ship doesn't come in,
    swim out to it!

Jonathan Winters

Some people follow their dreams,
    others hunt them down
    and beat them mercilessly
    into submission.

Neil Kendall

When a man
        asks *himself*
            what is meant
      by *action,*
    he proves that
        he *isn't* a man
          of *action.*
  Action
      is a LACK of
             BALANCE.
In order to *act*
      you **must**
          be SOMEWHAT INSANE.
A reasonably *sensible man*
     is satisfied with
            thinking.

            Georges Clemenceau

· D O ·

Just as a flower which seems beautiful
and has color but no perfume,
so are the fruitless words
of the man who speaks them
but does them not.

Dhammapada

All speech is vain and empty
unless it be accompanied by action.

Demosthenes

You can commit no greater folly
than to sit by the road side
until someone comes along
and invites you to ride with him
to wealth or influence.

John B. Gough

142

· D O ·

Look **not**
   mournfully
      into the *past*.
It comes **not**
      BACK again.
   Wisely
      improve
         the present.
It is *thine*.
   Go forth
      TO MEET
   the shadowy
      future,
         without
            fear.

Henry Wadsworth Longfellow

Taking a new step, uttering a new word,
  is what people fear most.

Fyodor Dostoevski

Hope in every sphere of life
  is a privilege
  that attaches to action.
  No action, no hope.

Peter Levi

I do not believe in a fate
  that falls on men
  however they act,
  but I do believe in a fate
  that falls on men
  unless they act.

G. K. Chesterton

Somebody
should tell us,
right at the START
of *our lives*,
that we are **dying**.
Then we might *live*
life to
the L I M I T,
every minute
of *every* day.
Do it!
I say.
Whatever you
WANT to do,
do it now!
There are *only*
so many TOMORROWS.

Michael Landon

The bitterest tears shed over graves
   are for words left unsaid
   and deeds left undone.

Harriet Beecher Stowe

Iron rusts from disuse;
   stagnant water loses its purity
   and in cold weather becomes frozen;
   even so does inaction
   sap the vigor of the mind.

Leonardo da Vinci

Surrender is essentially
   an operation by means of
   which we set about explaining
   instead of acting.

Charles Péguy

KNOW
  the value of TIME;
    snatch,
      seize,
  and **enjoy**
      EVERY MOMENT of it.
No *idleness*,
    NO de l a y,
      NO *procrastination*;
NEVER PUT OFF
    until tomorrow
  what
    you can *do*
        today.

Earl of Chesterfield

No one will do it for you.

Ben Stein

Nobody ever drowns
by falling in water.
They drown
by staying there.

Zig Zigler

No one is any better than you,
but you are no better
than anyone else
until you do something
to prove it.

Donald Laird

I am only **one**,
but still *I am one.*
I cannot do
EVERYTHING,
but **still**
I can do
SOMETHING;
and because
I cannot do
EVERYTHING
I will not refuse
to do
the SOMETHING
that
I can do.

Helen Keller

Whatever fortune brings,
   don't be afraid of doing things.

A. A. Milne

The few who do
   are the envy of the many
   who only watch.

Jim Rohn

One of the earliest lessons
   I learned as a child was that
   if you looked away from something,
   it might not be there
   when you looked back.

John Edgar Wideman

To bring
one's self
to a *frame of mind*
and to the proper
energy
to ACCOMPLISH things
that **require**
plain *hard work*
C O N T I N U O U S L Y
is the one
big battle
that *everyone* has.
When *this battle*
is WON for all time,
then **everything**
is *easy.*

Thomas A. Buckner